Ida B. Wells
Let the Truth Be Told

BY WALTER DEAN MYERS
ILLUSTRATED BY BONNIE CHRISTENSEN

Amistad
Collins

An Imprint of HarperCollinsPublishers

Ida Bell Wells was born on the sixteenth of July, 1862, in Holly Springs, Mississippi. The first child of James Wells and his wife, Elizabeth, was beautiful, bright eyed, and healthy. Still, there was much to worry about. James Wells, although a skilled carpenter, was legally a slave, and so was his wife. Three years later, the Constitution of the United States was changed. The Thirteenth Amendment made slavery illegal. All the black people of Holly Springs were now free.

Over the next few years young Ida was joined by three brothers and three sisters. The Wells children were taught to be responsible for one another and the family home. Each child had chores to do around the house. When the Methodists started a school in Holly Springs, James Wells made sure that his children attended.

"Our job was to go to school and learn all we could," Ida would say later.

"My mother went along to school with us until she learned to read the Bible. After that she visited the school regularly to see how we were getting along."

—from *The Crusade for Justice: The Autobiography of Ida B. Wells*

Encouraged by both of her parents, Ida became a good student. She could handle schoolwork better even than some of the adults, who were just learning to read after a lifetime of working in the cotton fields.

But Ida saw that life was not good for all black people. There were places black people could not enter and jobs they could not get. If blacks were accused of crimes, they often would not get a trial. Some were even killed by angry white mobs. When a person was killed in this manner, it was called lynching. Ida saw the sadness and fear caused by the lynchings.

FIFTH VOLUME

RIDDLED

The Mob's Summary Execution of the Three Negro Prisoners.

Taken to An Old Field and Filled With Shot.

In 1877 sixteen-year-old Ida was visiting her grandmother in another part of Mississippi when she learned that yellow fever had struck Holly Springs. Both of Ida's parents and her youngest brother died.

Heartbroken, Ida returned home. She listened as the family's neighbors and friends talked about what they could do to help raise the Wells children. "That won't be necessary." Ida stood up as tall as her five feet allowed. "I can take care of my family."

It wouldn't be easy, Ida knew. They could live in the house that her parents had owned and would have the small savings that James Wells had carefully put aside.

Ida decided to take a test to become a teacher. She had no experience teaching, but she had helped her sisters and brothers with their lessons. After passing the test, Ida taught in a small town six miles away from Holly Springs. A friend of the family agreed to keep the smaller children while Ida worked.

Ida taught during the week and came home on weekends to do the washing and ironing for her brothers and sisters. Each Sunday night Ida would ride back to the country school on an old mule. She worked in small schools around Holly Springs for two and a half years.

Ida's aunt Fannie lived in Memphis, Tennessee, forty-three miles north of Holly Springs. There were more teaching opportunities there, and in 1881 Ida, now nineteen, moved to Memphis with two of her sisters.

Teaching was just as hard there. Ida had to travel by train to get to her job. She often used the time on the train to read or write letters. She read newspapers and whatever books she could find. She also began to keep a diary.

One day Ida took a seat in the ladies' coach of the train. The conductor refused to take her ticket and told her to move to the smoking car. Ida knew that the conductor wanted her to move because she was black. She refused.

The conductor tried to pull her out of the seat. Ida was small. She braced her feet against the seat in front. When the conductor put his hand on her arm, she bit him.

The conductor got two strong men, and together they dragged Ida from the car. Ida, very upset, left the train and went back to Memphis.

Ida decided to sue the railroad. She won her case in court and was awarded five hundred dollars. The local newspaper, the *Memphis Appeal-Avalanche,* ran the story. The headline read "Darky Damsel Gets Damages." Ida also wrote about the incident for her church paper, *The Living Way.*

"Judge Pierce, who was an ex-union soldier from Minnesota, awarded me damages of five hundred dollars."
—from *The Crusade for Justice: The Autobiography of Ida B. Wells*

Later the court's decision was reversed, and Ida did not receive the money she had won in court. But she did see how people reacted to the article she had written. Ida continued to write for her church paper, and soon black newspapers around the country began to carry her essays. She wrote under the name "Iola" and was called the "Princess of the Press." T. Thomas Fortune, the noted New York publisher of the *New York Age,* wrote:

> *She has become famous as one of the few of our women who handle a goose quill with diamond point as easily as any man in newspaper work. If Iola were a man she would be a humming independent in politics. She has plenty of nerve and is as sharp as a steel trap.*

By 1889 Ida had stopped teaching and wrote full-time. She even became part owner of a newspaper called *Free Speech and Headlight.* In August 1892 both her sharp pen and her nerve would be put to the test.

The People's Grocery Store was owned by three of Ida's friends. A dispute occurred between the three and some white men who did not like the idea that black men owned the store. A fight ensued, and shots were exchanged.

The next morning hundreds of black men were arrested, including Ida's friends. Several days later the store owners were taken from the jail by a white mob and murdered. Ida was filled with grief and anger. She knew that the deaths of black men were often ignored. Longing for justice, Ida turned to the only weapon she had, her writing.

In her articles for *Free Speech and Headlight* Ida urged the black people of Memphis to leave town or stop supporting white businesses or riding the white-owned streetcar line. Ida Wells had organized one of the first economic boycotts. She was threatened, and her friends feared for her life.

When Ida left town to visit New York, her office was invaded by hoodlums and destroyed.

"This is what opened my eyes to what lynching really was. An excuse to get rid of Negroes who were acquiring wealth and property."
—from *The Crusade for Justice: The Autobiography of Ida B. Wells*

Ida was forced to leave Memphis, but she was determined not to be quiet or fearful. She began writing for the *New York Age* from her new home in Chicago. Her articles exposed the poor treatment of black people, especially black men. More than any other person in America, she spoke and wrote about the crime of lynching. She believed that all Americans, black and white, were entitled to equal justice.

In 1893 she published a book on lynching titled *The Red Record*. Her good friend Frederick Douglass wrote an introduction to the book.

Dear Miss Wells,
*   …Brave woman! You have done your people and mine a service which can neither be weighed nor measured.*

Ida was invited to speak in England and Scotland. She spoke with eloquence and passion about the unfair treatment of black men.

"In the past ten years over a thousand black men and women and children have met this violent death at the hands of a white mob. And the rest of America has remained silent."

—letter from Ida B. Wells to the editor of the Birmingham (England) *Daily Post*, published May 16, 1893; from *The Crusade for Justice: The Autobiography of Ida B. Wells*

JANE ADDAMS

SUSAN B. ANTHONY

In June 1895 Ida B. Wells married Ferdinand Lee Barnett, an attorney and newspaper publisher. Susan B. Anthony, who fought so hard for women's rights, worried that Ida would give up her life as a crusader for justice. Ida replied, "Miss Anthony, don't you believe in women getting married?" She said, "Oh, yes, but not women like you who had a special call for special work. . . . I know of no one in this country better fitted to do the work you had in hand than yourself."

Although she was raising her own family, Ida Wells did not abandon her role as a fighter. In 1900 the *Chicago Tribune* ran a series of articles recommending school segregation. Ida asked for help from another brave warrior in the fight for social equality, Jane Addams. Miss Addams brought together a group of influential white businesspeople to hear Ida plead her case. Ida Wells convinced them to help keep Chicago schools open for all children.

Although a wife and mother, Ida continued to write and organize. In 1909 she was one of the major speakers and organizers of the group that would eventually call itself the National Association for the Advancement of Colored People. Ida Wells understood that among African Americans there were important differences. Those who were powerful and doing well often weren't willing to make a commitment to help the poorest among them. They wanted to be "respectable."

Ida Wells also wanted to be respectable but felt it was her duty to fight for justice. "I'd rather go down in history as one lone Negro who dared to tell the government that it has done a dastardly thing than to save my skin by taking back what I have said."

Ida continued her fight for justice by taking up the cause of suffrage—her friend Susan B. Anthony's lifelong mission. After talking to Anthony about voting rights, Ida was convinced that women's suffrage was critical to political change for black women. In 1913 Ida created the Alpha Suffrage Club. It was the first voting organization for black women in the state of Illinois.

At Woodrow Wilson's presidential inauguration in 1913, Ida and five thousand other women marched for the right to vote. When white suffragists asked Ida to march in the separate colored section, Ida sternly refused. It took several more years of hard work by Ida and many others, but women finally won the right to vote in 1920.

Ida Wells spoke up for what she believed. Her weapons were her keen mind and her pen. Leaders as different as W.E.B. DuBois and Marcus Garvey, the black nationalist, consulted her. In 1930, feeling that the candidates for the state legislature in Illinois were not doing enough for the people, she ran for the state senate. She did not win the race, but again her clear and passionate voice was heard.

The following year, on the twenty-fifth of March, Ida B. Wells died. For more than a half century this dynamic, intelligent woman used her writing skills to promote freedom, safety, and justice. She made America a better place.

TIMELINE

1861   The Civil War begins when Confederate forces attack Fort Sumter in Charleston, South Carolina, on April 12. Eleven states will secede from the Union to form the Confederate States of America.

1862   Ida Bell Wells is born in Holly Springs, Mississippi. Since her parents are slaves, by law Ida is born into slavery.

1863   President Abraham Lincoln issues the Emancipation Proclamation on New Year's Day, which frees all the slaves in rebel states.

1865   On April 9 Gen. Robert E. Lee surrenders his Confederate Army to Gen. Ulysses S. Grant at Appomattox Court House in Virginia. Slavery is abolished by the Thirteenth Amendment to the Constitution on December 6.

1877   Federal troops are removed from the South, and Reconstruction ends. The South begins to pass Jim Crow laws.

1878   Yellow fever hits Mississippi, including Holly Springs. James and Elizabeth Wells are victims. Ida becomes the head of the family.

1879   Ida begins teaching in Mississippi while trying to keep the Wells family together.

1881   Ida moves to Memphis, Tennessee, with two of her sisters.

1884   Ida sues the Chesapeake and Ohio Railroad Company for forcing her to sit in a smoking car when she had paid for a first class ticket.

1885   Ida begins writing articles for *The Living Way* under the pen name "Iola."

1889   Ida becomes editor and part owner of *Free Speech and Headlight*.

SECOND VOLUME   MEMPHIS, JULY 15, 1889   FIVE CENTS

1892	After three friends are murdered in a racial incident, Ida dedicates herself to educating Americans about the horrors of lynching. Ida writes her first pamphlet about lynching, called "Southern Horrors: Lynch Law in All Its Phases."
1893	Ida moves to Chicago after a mob destroys the *Free Speech and Headlight* offices and threatens to lynch her. She becomes an owner and editor of *New York Age*.
1893	Ida delivers a series of lectures on lynchings in Great Britain, raising worldwide awareness of these atrocities.
1895	Ida marries Ferdinand Lee Barnett and purchases her husband's newspaper, *The Conservator*.
1896	Ida helps found the National Association of Colored Women. U.S. Supreme Court rules that segregation is legal in *Plessy v. Ferguson*.
1910	Ida Wells-Barnett works with W.E.B. DuBois and others to begin the National Association for the Advancement of Colored People (NAACP). She is not active in the organization.
1920	The Nineteenth Amendment is ratified, giving women the right to vote.
1930	Ida runs for the Illinois state senate and campaigns fiercely but loses.
1931	Ida dies in Chicago at the age of sixty-eight.
1990	A U.S. postage stamp of Ida is created for the United States Postal Service's Black Heritage series

THE WORDS OF IDA B. WELLS

"Our job was to go to school and learn all we could."

"Judge Pierce, who was an ex-union soldier from Minnesota, awarded me damages of five hundred dollars."

"In the past ten years over a thousand black men and women and children have met this violent death at the hands of a white mob. And the rest of America has remained silent."

"My mother went along to school with us until she learned to read the Bible. After that she visited the school regularly to see how we were getting along."

"That won't be necessary. I can take care of my family."

"This is what opened my eyes to what lynching really was. An excuse to get rid of Negroes who were acquiring wealth and property."

"Miss Anthony, don't you believe in women getting married?"

"I'd rather go down in history as one lone Negro who dared to tell the government that it has done a dastardly thing than to save my skin by taking back what I have said."

For Diane Foulds
—B.C.

"She has plenty of nerve and is as sharp as a steel trap."
—T. Thomas Fortune, publisher of the *New York Age*

Amistad and Collins are imprints of HarperCollins Publishers.

Ida B. Wells: Let the Truth Be Told   Text copyright © 2008 by Walter Dean Myers   Illustrations copyright © 2008 by Bonnie Christensen
Manufactured in China. All rights reserved. No part of this book may be used or reproduced in any manner whatsoever without written permission except in the case of brief quotations embodied in critical articles and reviews. For information address HarperCollins Children's Books, a division of HarperCollins Publishers, 1350 Avenue of the Americas, New York, NY 10019.   www.harpercollinschildrens.com

Library of Congress Cataloging-in-Publication Data
Myers, Walter Dean, date Ida B. Wells : let the truth be told / by Walter Dean Myers ; illustrated by Bonnie Christensen. — 1st ed.   p.   cm.
ISBN 978-0-06-027705-5 (trade bdg.)   ISBN 978-0-06-027706-2 (lib. bdg.)   1. Wells-Barnett, Ida B., 1862–1931—Juvenile literature.   2. African American women civil rights workers—Biography—Juvenile literature.   3. Civil rights workers—United States—Biography—Juvenile literature.   4. African American women journalists—Biography—Juvenile literature.   5. African American women educators—Biography—Juvenile literature. 6. African Americans—Biography—Juvenile literature. 7. United States—Race relations—Juvenile literature.   I. Christensen, Bonnie, ill.   II. Title.   E185.97.W55M94 2008   323.092—dc22   [B]   2007040107   CIP   AC
Designed by Stephanie Bart-Horvath   1 2 3 4 5 6 7 8 9 10 ❖ First Edition